IMAGES
of America

CHESTER

Taverns were opened on the two great roads which intersected at what is now the village of Chester. These roads were opened at a very early date, sometime before 1740. One was called the Landing Road and led from Brunswick Landing up to Sussex County. The other great road was called the Washington Turnpike and traveled from Morristown to the Pennsylvania country. The Chester Stage Coach had seats on each side and a step at the back, and was pulled by two horses. It ran between the village and the Muskrat Depot and met all trains until the 1920s. (J.T. Wyckoff Collection.)

IMAGES
of America

CHESTER

Joan S. Case

ARCADIA

First printed in 1998.

Published by Arcadia Publishing,
an imprint of Tempus Publishing, Inc.
2 Cumberland Street
Charleston, SC 29401

Printed in Great Britain.

Library of Congress Catalog Card Number: 98-86141

For all general information contact Arcadia Publishing at:
Telephone 843-853-2070
Fax 843-853-0044
E-Mail sales@arcadiapublishing.com

For customer service and orders:
Toll-Free 1-888-313-2665

Visit us on the internet at http://www.arcadiapublishing.com

The Weldon brothers left England and came to the region called Hacklebarney in 1739. They were mining men, and they built a dam in the stream at Lower Hacklebarney to furnish water power. It has been noted that they built this mill in order to exchange its products for the charcoal that farmers burned during the winter season. Also noted, in 1790, "the old mill was doing full duty and was a mecca for boys and men to exchange news of the countryside." (J.T. Wyckoff Collection.)

CONTENTS

Acknowledgments   6

Introduction   7

1.   Making a Living   9

2.   A Way of Life   25

3.   The Many Faces   41

4.   Home Sweet Home   55

5.   Church and State   71

6.   Reading, Writing, and . . .   81

7.   Always There When Needed   93

8.   Mails, Rails, and Down the Trails   109

ACKNOWLEDGMENTS

When I first started putting this book together, I sent out many letters asking for old photographs and any information on the history of Chester and its families. I would like to thank the many people who responded to the letters to let me know that they either had a few old photographs that I could take a look at, or those who just called to say they didn't have any photos but would help me out in any other way. To all of you—I thank you.

Throughout this work I give credit to the person who supplied the cleanest-quality photograph that would produce the best results in the book. There were so many wonderful people who took the time to sit down with me and tell me stories of old times in Chester, and I appreciate their cooperation and their enthusiasm for this project.

I would like to give a special thank-you to the following people—without their help this project would not have been a success: Georgia and Louis Case, Joyce Wyckoff, Carmen Smith, Ann Apgar, Len Taylor, Ken Caro, Gil Taylor Sr., Mary Parks, James "Reb" Hare, Eunice Lee, Clara Ammerman, Charlie and Ginny Breitweiser, Herman and Shirley Rademacher, Margaret Ardin, Doris Hoffman, Irene and Nancy Tiffenback, Charlotte Hoffman, Dawn Neil, Bob Horton, Cliff Waters, Bea Cowie, Cyrilla and Delmont Van Stone, Evelyn Beiser, Frank Carey, Howard Sutton Sr., Howard Sutton Jr., Charles Hardin, Martin Winkler, Lois "Tommy" Barker, and a very special thank you goes out to my uncle, John T. Wyckoff, who supplied not only many old photographs and history, but supplied me with a great deal of knowledge on photography.

Again, I thank you all, and promise that the next time I meet you on the street I will say "hello" instead of "do you have any old pictures of Chester?"

INTRODUCTION

Try to imagine what it was like over two hundred years ago. In the early 1700s, the trails across New Jersey were Native American trails, wide enough for only one man on horseback and densely wooded on every side. It was by these trails that a band of settlers from Southold and Easthampton, Long Island, came to the rolling, green hills of Morris County. Two of these trails crossed in the area that the Minisink Indians called "Alamatunk," which meant "black earth bottom," for Black River, which was the original name for Chester.

Most Chester people have said that no one knows why the name "Black River" was dropped and "Chester" adopted. Because Chester, England, was the home of their ancestors who had migrated to New England, and then to Southold and the Hamptons, and the grandsons of those ancestors who came to Black River, some of the residents had been calling their community "Chester" for a good while. It must have been a great satisfaction to the people of Black River to receive notice from the state that the wish to create their own township had been granted. So January 29, 1799, began the business of naming the new township Chester. The people of Chester will be celebrating their town's bicentennial in 1999.

Because of the two great roads previously mentioned, taverns, inns, blacksmith shops, and other travel-related businesses flourished during the latter half of the 18th century. Distilleries also did a thriving business in applejack and apple brandy (known as "Jersey Lightning"), produced from apples grown in the many local orchards—a few of which still operate today. Not only were the rolling hills of the area dotted with the orchards of peaches and apples, but dairy and sheep farming were very widespread.

During early settlement, agriculture was the mainstay of the area; however, industrial potential was soon to be realized. Numerous swift-flowing streams provided ideal settings for water-powered grist- and sawmills. These streams also served as sources of power for the early charcoal-burning forges and furnaces which were used to work the iron ore taken from local mines. The Civil War brought more demands for iron and the mines began to flourish. During the period from the late 1860s to the late 1880s, Chester had 28 active mines. In 1880, six mines were operating on Main Street alone. Several hundred thousand tons of iron ore were taken from 25 to 30 different mines at this time. In 1868, the Lackawanna Railroad built its branch in Chester, and in 1872–73, tracks were laid to connect it with the Hedges and Hacklebarney mines. These tracks were later purchased by the Central Railroad and carried through to High Bridge. Later on, the D.L. & W. Railroad took over the tracks alongside Chester's "Muskrat" Station, that ran to Dover.

Chester's iron industry suffered with the mining of much larger and richer iron ore deposits found in Minnesota's Mesabi Range. By the 1890s, all of the mines were shut down. Residents who could not return to farming soon moved away. But even though Chester died as a mill and mining town, some unusual light industry moved in to support the town. Some of this new industry was the Sturzenegger's Swiss Embroidery Factory from New York and the Davidson Handkerchief Factory. Also in the early 1900s, Chester became a very popular retreat for city-weary New Yorkers because of the local hotels that charged reasonable rates and the chance to visit the famous springs, with their health-giving waters, on top of Schooley's Mountain.

Effort has been put forth to group this pictorial history of Chester into ways of life that were important to the people of the area. The small towns of those days needed their main street with all the local businesses, as well as the schools, churches, homes, and families. The local taverns were not only a stopping-off place for people to "wet their whistle," but it was where a lot of the news of the area was passed on. A lot of these old buildings still stand on our main street and country roads today, and with this group of images, I will try to show what it was like back in the late 1800s through the mid-1900s.

It has been such an enjoyable and exciting time talking to the families who have lived in Chester for generations. They were so wonderful to dig through all of their old photographs, clippings, and postcards. I have learned so much more about the town in which my family has lived for two hundred years now, thanks to all of these people. I have given credit to the person or group who supplied the image, and since many of the same images were donated by different people, I have used and credited the clearest one, and the one that would reproduce the best.

So please step back in time with me and wander down the streets. Stop into the taverns and general store. Visit with the families in their homes and walk with them in their daily lives, and listen to the whistle of the trains here in my home town, Chester, and remember the simpler, quiet life way back when.

One
MAKING A LIVING

Gilbert Y. Hopler had been a successful and popular owner of this general store, but became the victim of Chester's only hold-up/murder. Two men entered the store and demanded his money. He refused and they shot him. On the back of this postcard, dated 1913, there was a note from Ella Hopler to Mrs. John S. Wyckoff for the prices of linoleum ($1 a running yard) and for brass binding (5¢ a yard). (Beatrice Wyckoff Case.)

Isaiah Younglove, who had a gristmill at Milltown, was serving in 1760 as a county judge. He put up for sale, in 1761, his gristmill with 160 acres on Black River. That mill, at a later date, burned down, and this present mill now stands in its place (built in 1826). Cooper Mill served the local community throughout the 1800s, as local residents brought their grain to be ground at the mill, which was powered by the water of the Black River. The mill was closed in 1913, and the Morris County Park Commission purchased the property in 1963. They have restored the mill and have it in operation today for their many visitors. (John T. Wyckoff collection.)

John P. Rockefeller had been at the Milldale (Milltown) store for several years. One corner of the store was for a branch post office, and Oliver Van Fleet brought the mail on a bicycle every day from the Chester Post Office. Mr. Rockefeller stored his perishables in a spring that ran beneath the store. Bills were frequently paid with eggs, butter, produce, etc. Unfortunately, the store burned down on January 31, 1913, and the Old Mill Tavern now stands on the old foundation. (Margaret Ardin.)

Fred Jenkins had sold his drug business to Lon Green and the printing shop which he had opened in the store on the west side to George E. Conover. Mr. Conover put his paint and wallpaper business in the front and operated the printing business, calling it "The Conover Press," in the rear. Many of the photographs in this book are thanks to Mr. Conover. The post office was also in this store in the 1890s, with Billie Dee as the postmaster in 1897. Pictured is Lon Green in the middle, and to his right is Alvah Barker. (John T. Wyckoff collection.)

One advertisement for Green's Pharmacy read, "Alonzo P. Green—Purveyor of pure drugs and medicines and prescriptions carefully compounded." George Conover and Alonzo P. Green organized the Chester Telephone Company, beginning as a two-phone line between the drug store and the railroad station at Muskrat. The switchboard was in the back room of the drugstore. Pictured behind the counter is Lon Green. (Ken Urban.)

11

Billie Dee lived all of his life on Main Street in Chester. He owned a store that was a confectionery store with newspapers and tobacco, which his wife ran. Billie Dee is most remembered for his ball-playing and his claim to fame is that—and apparently a *Newark News* sports reporter believed it—he had pitched the very first "curve ball" in baseball, in 1881, by accident. His story to the reporter was that his "finger caught in a torn seam and the result was an amazing out-curve." Pictured is Billie Dee. (Ginny and Charlie Breitweiser.)

Thomas Bryant Stout and his wife, Deborah Terry, had inherited an old white farmhouse and according to the Shields 1853 Map, Mr. Stout also owned the Crossroads Inn, a house, and a blacksmith shop, on Fairmount Avenue. Pictured here is the blacksmith shop, which was built in 1885. (John T. Wyckoff collection.)

This hotel was originally a farmhouse built in 1752. In 1779, Jacob Drake Jr. purchased it and turned it into a tavern and inn. It soon became a popular place for stage wagons to change horses, for social functions, and for holding local court days. It operated continuously as a tavern for the next 183 years until, sadly, it burned down on November 26, 1962. Some of the names it held over the years were "Jacob Drake's Tavern;" the "Crossroads Inn;" "Union Hotel;" the "Flagstaff Inn," and "Dean's Crossroads Hotel." (John T. Wyckoff collection.)

This is how "Dean's Crossroads Hotel" appeared just before it burned down in 1962. (Gilbert Taylor Sr.)

In this photograph we are looking west along Main Street around 1915. On the left is the Tippett-Masonic Building where Charles E. Tippett put a bottling plant in the basement in order to bottle Porter, ginger ale, root beer, and lemon and strawberry soda water. A barber shop and a pool room occupied the first floor and were operated by William Savage. (Chester Historical Society.)

Charles R. Hardin had come from Newton in Sussex County in 1854 to attend the Chester Institute. After finishing his schooling he remained to work as clerk in Daniel Budd's general store and he lived upstairs over the store. Later he erected this building east of the Chester House. It was intended for use as a bank but was never so used. The first floor of this building became Hardin's Clothing Store and the back end of the store was rented to James Tredway for his carriage shop. (Charles Hardin.)

On May 12, 1810, Isaiah Fairclo sold this lot to 22-year-old Zephaniah Drake and his father, Jacob Drake Jr. Here Zephaniah erected the "Brick Tavern," which was more elegant than earlier taverns in the Chester area. The Drake's hotel was the place to buy stagecoach tickets for the trip to New York and a favorite stop for refreshment and change of horses. (Ken Urban.)

Here the "Brick Tavern," now called the "Chester House," was purchased by the Flemings in 1916. They operated it for many years, developing a dining room famous for its food—especially Long Island duck and chicken dinners. (John T. Wyckoff collection.)

James G. Case came to Chester in 1876 to manage a branch store of the "Richard Simpson Co. Stores." He was later made a partner, conducting the store as "Simpson & Case." In 1913, he took it over completely under the name "James G. Case." He and his family lived upstairs. (Ann Apgar.)

Here is the same building as above, but in the late 1920s and early '30s it was occupied by two different businesses. Fred L. De Hart ran a radio repair shop on the left, and on the right was George W. Ulrick's Luncheonette. (Ginny and Charlie Breitweiser.)

In the 1940s and '50s, this same building was transformed into "Leck's Luncheonette," where many of the people that I spoke to remembered fondly the rows of penny candies and sitting at the counter for ice cream sundaes. The building in the back was connected to the store by a plank walkway. (Ann Apgar.)

Here is an inside view of what the soda and radio shop looked like. This is where, many a night, townspeople would gather to get the local gossip and to play checkers. (Ginny and Charlie Breitweiser.)

This is a reversed print of the "Centennial Building," which was built for William J. Northrup in 1876 by the father of Long Valley's "Old Charlie Hall." In 1877, St. Mark's Episcopal Church of Mendham met at Northrup Hall on the second floor, which is now apartments. Some of the stores that occupied the first floor in early days were a paint store, a clothing store, a harness shop, a clock shop, and a butcher shop. (Chester Historical Society.)

Chester P. Apgar Jr. purchased the "Centennial Building" in 1945 and operated the hardware store at the east end. The borough municipal offices were located in the west end. Pictured here is Paul Apgar in front of his hardware store that he loved so much. (Ann Apgar.)

Thomas Topping came from Southampton in the 1750s or 1760s and was the first to own the property pictured above, shown here as the Maple Tree Inn (which operated in the mid-1900s). After the death, in 1777, of Topping, Dr. Joseph Hedges purchased the farm and most likely lived in the small, low wing at the eastern end of the inn. (Herman Rademacher.)

This is the same old farmhouse shown at the top of the page, only it was now called "The Wo Wanda." It started out as a restaurant in the mid-1940s and was first called "The Wo Wanda," then the "Maple Tree Inn," then "The Twins Inn," "Sweeney Todd's," and "The Lamplighter." (Ken Urban.)

"The Old Factory Building" has housed many businesses since 1844, when the Van Doren brothers manufactured threshing machines. Some of the other businesses were Daniel Budd's machine shop and Davidson's handkerchief manufacturing company. Pictured here is J.W. Arrowsmith, manufacturer of arch supports. (Ken Urban.)

H.P. Sanderson advertised, "Plumber-Gasfitter—manufacturer of and dealer in stoves, tinware, hardware, general house furnishings, goods, and furnaces." (Ken Urban.)

20

In the 1890s, Edmund Sturzenegger of New York City purchased property near the Muskrat Depot (D.L. & W. Station) from Isabella (Ming) Skellenger to build this brick building for his mother, Regina, in order for her to operate her Swiss embroidery factory. Sometime between 1892 and 1896, this fine brick building was erected by James Burr. (John T. Wyckoff collection.)

These were some of the workers at the new factory, where Swiss embroidery of various kinds was performed on slippers, dresses, badges, banners, and handkerchiefs. Some experienced workers from New York came to work for Mrs. Sturzenegger, and many local people also found employment with her. (John T. Wyckoff collection.)

This photo of workers and miners was taken at the Taylor Blast Furnace, located on Furnace Road. Regrettably, none of the workers have been identified. (John T. Wyckoff collection.)

The Chester Oil Company, who wholesaled fuel oils, gasoline, and kerosene, operated here at the intersection of Routes 206 and 24. There were also apartments and a restaurant operating in this building. In the mid-1960s, the building was renovated and the two "towers" were torn down. (John T. Wyckoff collection.)

The farmhouse, which is now the Larison Turkey Farm Inn, was built by Isaac Corwin about 1800. In 1829, James Topping bought it for $1,400, and in the 1940s, Willis Larison acquired the property and eventually turned it into the landmark restaurant that it is today. (Ken Urban.)

There always seems to be a line of people waiting to go into Larison's Turkey Farm, even in the 1960s. (Ann Apgar.)

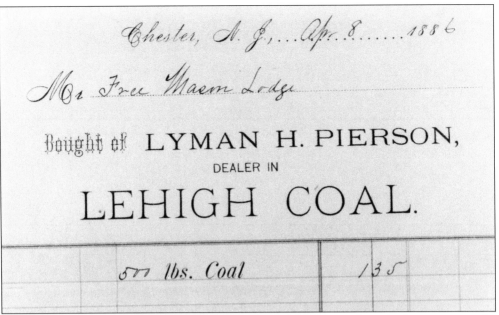

Chester, N. J., Apr. 8 1886

Mr Free Mason Lodge

Bought of **LYMAN H. PIERSON,**

DEALER IN

LEHIGH COAL.

500 lbs. Coal	135

Pictured here is a sales receipt for coal delivered to the Masonic Lodge, which was next to the Chester House. The coal yards were at the comer of Routes 206 and 24, near the Chester Railroad Station. Lyman Pierson lived on the hill opposite the coal yards. (Howard Sutton Jr.)

In 1906, Mr. William F. Parks purchased this farm, mainly as a dairy farm, but he also planted some apple and peach trees. This is where he raised his family, and pictured here is his son, Scott V. Parks, who learned farming from his father. This photograph, taken in the late 1960s, shows Scott V. Parks in front of the stand where the family still sells produce. (Mary Parks.)

Two

A WAY OF LIFE

Pictured here is Dr. William Woodhull Hedges and his wife, Jane English Hedges, playing a board game. Dr. Woodhull Hedges was the son of Dr. Joseph Hedges, and two of his nine children grew up to also be doctors, one of whom was to practice in Chester, as did the previous two generations of doctors. (John T. Wyckoff collection.)

This photograph is looking east on Main Street. Some of the businesses that can be seen are the Chester House on the left and, next to that, the Hardin-Masonic Building. Over on the right side of the photograph is the De Hart radio shop and the Ulrick Luncheonette. (Joan S. Case.)

Hunting played a very large part in many of the families around the Chester area. Most of the hunters raised and trained their own dogs. Pictured here was an avid hunter named George Washington Wyckoff. The photo was probably taken around 1918. (Joan S. Case.)

Pictured here is one of the many ponds in the Chester area that would be used for cutting ice, for fishing, and for ice skating. This was the Simpson's Pond, located on the corner by the Sturzenegger's Embroidery Factory. (Ann Apgar.)

Most families in the Chester area were farmers and had to plow their fields with the help of their horses. This is a scene near Chester which is believed to be near Pleasant Hill. (Gilbert Taylor Sr.)

George Conover had occupied the store at the west end of Lon Green's building for many years, operating a printing shop, a paint and paper-hanging business, and, lastly, a general store. In 1919, he introduced to Chester what he called "a new way of shopping—cash and carry, with no monthly bills to pay." He also started a three-year publication of a monthly news sheet entitled *Conover Cash Store News*. (John T. Wyckoff collection.)

In 1901, Conover and Green organized the Chester Telephone Company, and it was located in the back room of the drug store. Pictured here is one of the telephone operators. (John T. Wyckoff collection.)

Here is a beautiful view of "Muskrat Valley" looking north. The large building was the Sturzenegger Embroidery Factory, and to the left of the factory was the Chester Railroad Station. Directly above is "Pleasant Hill Farm," and at the top right is the road going toward Pleasant Hill Cemetery. (Ann Apgar.)

The river for which the town of Chester was originally named (Black River) winds its way through the area giving power to the mills, fish for the fishermen, and pleasure for the boaters. It was a much wider river years ago. (Chester Historical Society.)

Here we see another view of Main Street with the Chester House and the Simpson and Case Store. Notice the telegraph pole and the large liberty pole standing in the grass area. During the Civil War, the custom of erecting "liberty poles" was revived throughout the state. Chester received one, complete with flag, from William E. Collis. This liberty pole was to stand until 1914, when it was taken down because of decay. (Chester Historical Society.)

This section of the Black River, which flows through Hacklebarney State Park, is called "Little Niagara." (Chester Historical Society.)

This is Henry Leck with his son Charlie on a sled in front of Leck's Luncheonette. (John T. Wyckoff collection.)

This is a tower built on "Telegraph Hill" by Boy Scout Troop Number One. The young man on the lowest step is Dink Reinhardt. The photograph was taken in the mid-1930s. (Herman Rademacher.)

This is a view of the Theo B. Wortman homestead along Pottersville Road. The Wortmans owned, in 1899, a rich and well-cultivated farm of 224 acres, largely planted with peaches. The orchards were said to be unsurpassed in the county. (Dorothy Metzler.)

This is what the center of Chester looked like in the early part of the century. Notice the "silent policeman" to the left of the boy on the bike. It was known to be knocked over on occasion by some of the locals on their way home from the taverns. (Ginny and Charlie Breitweiser.)

Leck's Luncheonette was where many of the local folks gathered to hear some of the town's news. A few that have been identified are, from left to right: (bottom row) Fred Wyckoff, Art Thompson, and Sara Thompson; (back row) third from the left is George Wyckoff, and the last two are Henry and Mildred Leck.

This is a view of a local dairy farm in Chester. (Ann Apgar.)

This is the original dam along the Black River at the location of the Cooper Grist Mill. (John T. Wyckoff.)

The Stroud family had wonderful views up on top of Pleasant Hill in the earlier part of this century. The view from here is looking over what is now the Black River Wildlife Management Area. (Pauline Stroud.)

This is a winter view of Main Street in the 1940s, looking west. (John T. Wyckoff collection.)

The Hacklebarney Pond was the home for this icehouse. The ice was cut in large blocks and carried out on wagons. (John T. Wyckoff collection.)

Here we see an aerial view of the Scott V. Parks farm along route 24. Taking care of the land was an important part of the farmer's life, as we see here in this photograph with the erosion control measures that Mr. Parks has taken. (Mary Parks.)

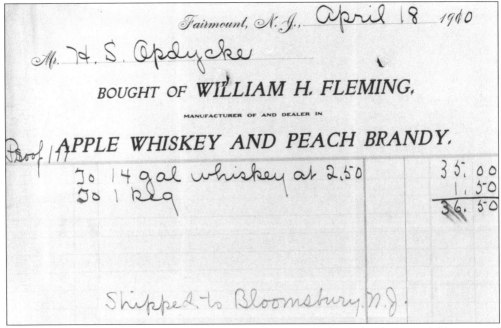

Fairmount, N. J., April 18 1910

Mr. H. S. Opdycke

BOUGHT OF **WILLIAM H. FLEMING,**

MANUFACTURER OF AND DEALER IN

Proof 111 *APPLE WHISKEY AND PEACH BRANDY.*

To 14 gal whiskey at 2.50		35.00
To 1 keg		1.50
		36.50

Shipped to Bloomsbury N. J.

As noted before, apples and peaches played an important role in the history of Chester and many of the towns surrounding the Chester area. Most of the produce was made into whiskey and brandy and shipped to other communities. (Howard Sutton Jr.)

Here some of the men of Chester are showing off their catch of the day from a deep-sea fishing trip. They have been identified from left to right as Art Thompson, Cecil Hoffman, Justin Russell, Bill Cramer, and Mahlon Pitney.

Around 1913, J. Augustus Drake was operating "Crystal Lake" (a dammed-up pond on Oakdale Road), supplying pure ice, the water for which emanated from springs. The now-vanished pond was also used for bathing, skating, and fishing by many of the people of the town. (Ann Apgar.)

Melrose Farms sat across the street from Crystal Lake and was mainly a chicken farm. It later became Grace Bible Chapel, and the surrounding farmland became a 40-home real estate development in the 1960s. (John T. Wyckoff.)

Black River was much wider then what we see today and was a source of recreation and enjoyment. (Chester Historical Society.)

In the 1960s, Grogan's Pond was where many of the children and adults from Chester spent their summer afternoons. Who could forget the snack bar, golf driving range, and the high diving board? A shopping center now occupies the spot. (Borough of Chester.)

This was one of the many locations that the Chester Post Office called home, and many years before it would have been Hopler's General Store. Now it is one of many antique craft-type stores that line the towns streets. (Borough of Chester.)

Pictured here is the Auberge Provencale Restaurant in the mid-1900s. Cut into one step leading down into the basement are the initials "WTB May 27, 1802." In 1810, Zephaniah Drake bought this property along with the tavern across Main Street which he operated while the Brick Hotel was being built. Daniel Budd lived here in the 1850s, and this is where the famous Chester Institute was opened. (Borough of Chester.)

Here again we see the old Hardin-Masonic Building, but in the mid-1900s it was home for a Taylor Rental store. Previous to this, many of the townspeople picked up their groceries at the IGA store that was located here. (Borough of Chester.)

Three

THE MANY FACES

The Rockefeller Band played at many Chester functions. Pictured here are: (seated) Joe (on the drums), Dorothy (on the piano), Elizabeth (on the guitar), and Della (on the mandolin); (standing) Arthur Jr. (on the trumpet), Arthur Sr. (on the violin), Charles (on the sax), and George (on the banjo). (George Apgar.)

About 1881, some of Chester's young adults formed the Chester Social and Literary Society. Meetings were "biweekly" and were held at the homes of the members. Every member was obliged to attend or pay a 5¢ fine. The program for each meeting consisted of literary, musical, and charade exercises. (John T. Wyckoff collection.)

This photo was shot before 1920, at the home of George and Cora Wyckoff on Cooper Lane, and they are pictured here. The Wyckoffs were known as hard workers—farming the land, hunting, and doing a lot of the mason-stone work we see around Chester today. (Joan S. Case.)

Because there were no local police, farmers in rural areas frequently had horses and other livestock stolen. This was especially true in New Jersey because of its convenient location between New York and Pennsylvania. Chester's "Vigilant and Protective Association" was organized in 1889. The object of the society was to protect the horses, mules, wagons, sleighs, and harnesses of its members; to assist owners in case of theft; and to reimburse owners in case of loss. (Frank Carey.)

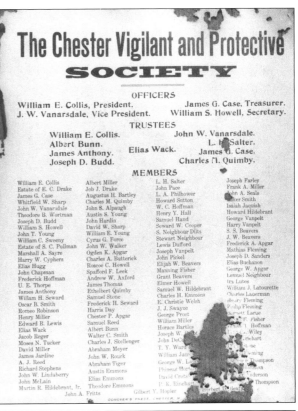

The Chester Vigilant and Protective
SOCIETY

OFFICERS

William E. Collis, President.   James G. Case, Treasurer.
J. W. Vanarsdale, Vice President.   William S. Howell, Secretary.

TRUSTEES

William E. Collis.   John W. Vanarsdale.
Albert Bunn.   L. H. Salter.
James Anthony.   Elias Wack.   James G. Case.
Joseph D. Budd.   Charles M. Quimby.

MEMBERS

William E. Collis	Albert Miller	L. H. Salter	Joseph Farley
Estate of E. C. Drake	Job J. Drake	John Pace	Frank A. Miller
James G. Case	Augustus H. Bartley	L. A. Philhower	John A. Seals
Whitfield W. Sharp	Charles M. Quimby	Howard Sutton	Asher Smith
John W. Vanarsdale	John S. Alpaugh	W. C. Hoffman	Isaiah Jaquish
Theodore B. Wortman	Austin S. Young	Henry Y. Hall	Howard Hildebrant
Joseph D. Budd	John Hardin	Samuel Hand	George Vanpelt
William S. Howell	David W. Sharp	Seward W. Cooper	Harry Vanpelt
John T. Young	William E. Young	S. Neighbour Diits	S. S. Beavers
William C. Sweeny	Cyrus G. Force	Stewart Neighbour	J. W. Beavers
Estate of S. C. Pullman	John W. Walker	Lewis Dufford	Frederick A. Apgar
Marshall A. Sayre	Ogden K. Apgar	Joseph Vanpelt	Mathias Fleming
Harry W. Cyphers	Charles A. Butterick	John Pickel	Joseph D. Sanders
Elias Hugg	Roscoe C. Howell	Elijah W. Beavers	Elias Buchanon
John Chapman	Spafford F. Leek	Manning Fisher	George W. Apgar
Frederick Hoffman	Andrew W. Axford	Grant Beavers	Lemuel Neighbour
U. E. Thorpe	James Thomas	Elmer Howell	Ira Lutes
James Anthony	Ethelbert Quimby	Samuel W. Hildebrant	William J. Latourette
Willam H. Seward	Samuel Stone	Charles H. Emmons	Charles Lauerman
Oscar B. Smith	Frederick H. Seward	E. Christie Welsh	Henry Fleming
Romeo Robinson	Harris Day	J. J. Swayze	Garrett Larue
Henry Miller	Chester P. Apgar	George Prost	F. Fisher
Edward B. Lewis	Samuel Reed	William Miller	Hoffman
Elias Wack	Albert Bunn	Horace Bartles	Wiley
Jacob Reger	Walter C. Smith	Joseph W.	Rinehart
Moses N. Tucker	Charles J. Skellenger	John DeC	Stone
David Miller	Abraham Meyer	T. Y. Ward	Deming
James Jardine	John W. Rourk	William Jam	Thompson
A. J. Reed	Abraham Tiger	George W. L	
Richard Stephens	Austin Emmons	Phineas Hort	Patterson
John W. Lindaberry	Elias Emmons	David Crota	Thompson
John McLain	Theodore Emmons	P. K. Rineha	
Martin R. Hildebrant, Jr.	John A. Fritts	Gilbert Y. Hopler	Herbert

CONOVER'S PRESS, CHESTER, N.

The Washington Camp Number Eight, patriotic order of the Sons of America, was organized by William E. Cary and George E. Conover and was instituted on August 5, 1895. In 1920, membership numbered nearly one hundred and included men of all professions and walks of life. They met in the upstairs of the building that is pictured (William Savage had his store on the ground floor). (John T. Wyckoff collection.)

General Nathan A. Cooper was born in 1801, and had many business interests in Chester, such as a farm, a brick yard, the Cooper Grist Mill, Cooper Mine, the first Milltown store, plus a great deal of acreage. He was very active in state military affairs, rising to general in 1854, in the New Jersey Cavalry, and from that day on he has been "General Cooper" to all of Chester. (John T. Wyckoff collection.)

In 1860, the Coopers built their "Mansion" on the road going to Ralston, and it was said that the house was never quite finished because of a difference of opinion as to the architecture. The General was a great lover of horses and a devotee of field sports. And, as the story goes, poor Mrs. Cooper was thrown from a carriage to the ground, but the General's first question was not for her safety, but which horse got to the crossroads first. (John T. Wyckoff collection.)

During World War II, some of Chester's "nurses" would wrap bandages in the Hardin-Masonic Building. A few of them have been identified as Mrs. Clara Sutton, Mrs. Tredway, Mrs. Rinehart, and Mrs. Searles. (Ann Apgar.)

Chester, as was the same in many towns, loved baseball. Pictured here is one of the teams that played in the area. (John T. Wyckoff collection.)

For entertainment, some of the townspeople would put on skits or plays in the municipal building. This one was a "Womenless Wedding," and was performed by all men, except for the two women (Caroline Smalley and Mrs. Austin Thompson) in the lower right-hand corner, who played the piano. Some of the men have been identified as John Croot (the bride), Chester Apgar (the groom), and Austin Thompson (the best man). A few others have been identified as Rev. Lemmon, Albert O'Brien, Ed Collis, Bill Tredway, Alvin Van Fleet, Justin Russell, Bobby Cramer, Walter Barkman, and Dink Rinehart. (Cyrilla and Delmont Van Stone.)

This photograph, taken in 1921, shows Edward Pickle and Beatrice Wyckoff standing in front of Daniel H. Skellinger's general store. He advertised groceries, dry goods, clothing, confectionery, provisions, and vegetables. His wife was storekeeper from 1895 until she retired in 1949. (Joan S. Case.)

The Chester Cornet Band was organized with Pierce Chamberlain as the leader, and some of the members are reported to be George E. Conover, William Coon, Charles Wack, William Frost, Herbert Conover, William Savage, Robert Vanover, Roscoe Howell, Frank Huston, Nelson Alpaugh, Albert and Charles Skellenger, and Fred Sharp. (Ken Urban.)

This photograph, taken around 1944 in front of where Lon Green had his pharmacy, shows a typical scene on a summer day along Main Street in Chester. All of the people have been identified. The two gentlemen seated in the center are Bill Smith (left) and John Rockefeller. The two women pictured at right are Mae Scheld (in the hat) and Caroline Smalley. On the far left, leaning against the post, is Gordon Barker. The boy on the bike is Walt Conklin, and the woman on the steps is Ada Myers, with her little brother Henry. The man seated on the first step is Doug Fleming, and the man with the dog is Burt Masker, with his pet "Zombie." The older gentleman sitting on the far left of the bench is Sam Ammerman. (Doris Hoffman.)

Pictured here are "Chester's Twins," Mae Rockefeller Stelce Conklin (who lived until the age of 101) and Mabel Rockefeller Hoffman (who lived until the age of 102). The man pictured with them is Owen Grour. (Doris Hoffman.)

George Conover and Alonzo Green organized the Chester Telephone Company in 1901. The switchboard was in the back room of Green's Drug Store. Pictured here are five of the telephone operators. From left to right are Helen Seger, Cyrilla Barkman Van Stone, Muriel Conklin, Beatrice Wyckoff Case, and Winnie Mansfield. (Joan S. Case.)

Mr. John P. Rockefeller, in 1898, rented the Milltown store and the house next to it from James Vanderveer and then bought the general store business from Warren Langdon. He drove a delivery wagon with a canvas top, and there was a coach dog running along behind. This went on for some 15 years, until the store was destroyed by fire. Now the "Old Mill Tavern" stands in its place. Pictured here are Mr. and Mrs. Rockefeller. (Doris Hoffman.)

This photo is of Mr. Scott V. Parks standing in front of the pond on the Parks Farm that he loved so much. (Mary Parks.)

John Steinberg thought up the idea of an honor roll to be placed in the center of town, with 110 names of men and women in the service from the borough and the township. The honor roll was painted by Mrs. Dorothy Morton and unveiled by Mrs. Austin Thompson and Mrs. Joseph Bragg. (Ann Apgar.)

In the late 1940s and early 1950s, when our boys were away in the service and gas was being rationed, Mr. Wrigley from Chicago decided people needed some sort of recreation. And since the stadiums were not being used, they decided to put together professional womens' baseball teams. Chester's own Lois "Tommy" Barker was one such ball player in 1950, and played for the "Grand Rapids Chicks." Her name, as well as those of other players, are currently listed in Baseball's Hall of Fame. (Lois "Tommy" Barker.)

Pictured here is Mrs. Adalene P. Searles, in 1959, on her 90th birthday. Elmer Searles came to Chester from East Orange and purchased the large white house near the crossroads and called it "Robin Hurst," because it attracted so many robins. (Bea Cowie.)

In this portrait we have Harold and Olive Searles Waters. Olive is the daughter of Elmer and Adalene Searles, mentioned above. (Cliff Waters.)

In 1951, the schoolchildren of Chester made contact with schoolchildren in Kumrovec, Yugoslavia. On April 5, "Kumrovec Day," Chester boys and girls took pencils, erasers, pads, and pictures of themselves to school, and a delegation of people of Slavic ancestry came to Chester to tour the town and take the gifts back to the children in Yugoslavia. The picture here was part of the program, and the men are, from left to right, Milton Emmons, William Cowie, Arnold Nichols, and Kimber McWilliams. (Bea Cowie.)

Pictured at the "roaster," at the end of Williamson Lane, are Beatrice Wyckoff Case and Dorothy Rogallsky—the photo was taken in the 1930s. Roasters were in use during the mining era so that the iron would be usable. (Joan S. Case.)

Posing along Main Street are, from left to right, Muriel Conklin Lutz, Cyrilla Barkman Van Stone, and Clara Mae Barkman Alpaugh. (Joan S. Case.)

The Winkler family grew up and worked on the farm property of Alfred G. Kay on Pottersville Road. Pictured here are Martin Winkler Sr. and five of his six children; from left to right are Mary, Helen, Margaret, Albert, Martin Jr., and their dog "Fhu." (Martin Winkler Jr.)

In this photograph, we see Reverend Zezzo (from the First Congregational Church) posing with his men's bible class. Some of the men have been identified as Howard Sutton, Bus Crum, Charles Rinehart, Ken O'Dell, Harvey Guerin, Willis Larison, Ken Dean, Tom Dean, Ed Collis, Paul Apgar, Lawrence Van Fleet, and Chris Christiansen. (Howard Sutton Sr.)

Beatrice Wyckoff, Cyrilla Barkman, and Lorraine Emmons are about to go skiing with friends—but before they do, they pose for a photograph in front of Emmons's garage on Hillside Road. (Joan S. Case.)

Four
HOME SWEET HOME

Dr Woodhull Hedges, son of Dr. Joseph Hedges, bought this farmhouse in 1821 and enlarged it by adding on the large east wing. He and his son, Dr. Smith Hedges, were active in the commercial development of the village. Pictured here are Dr. and Mrs. Smith Hedges and their son on the porch of the farmhouse, across from the Congregational church. (John T. Wyckoff collection.)

This is the front view of the Budd Mansion, built in 1869 by Daniel Budd. He built this fine, stone, 26-room house on "New Street" for the use of the Chester Institute, and as a home for his family. It was a spacious, three-story house with a bell tower. In its later years it served as the Mangel's home, as a business of candy making, and also as a rest home called the Chester Retreat. (Borough of Chester.)

In the 1700s, Walter Brown was one of the earlier settlers to Chester and owned the property down the Landing Road, which today is known as the corner of Pottersville Road and Old Chester Road. A relative of his, Peter Brown, opened a tavern on this corner, and it eventually became the farm of Charles R. Hardin. The Hardin family also owned the Hardin Store on Main Street in the mid-1800s. This is how the tavern looked as a home. In 1922, the porch area was built in. (Chester Historical Society.)

Caleb Horton, in 1748, came from Southold and bought 1,728 acres in the northeast area of Chester. At one time there were so many Hortons living in that area that it came to be known as "Hortontown." This is a photograph of the Horton's log home, which was situated near the same area as the Forest Hill School. (Bob Horton.)

Pictured here is one of the oldest buildings along Main Street, the western portion having been built in the 18th century. This was also home to Billie Dee's store. (Chester Historical Society.)

This home, called "Sunnyside," was built around 1880 by cabinetmaker James Topping for his widowed daughter-in-law, Nellie Topping, and her daughter Leila. Years later, as Miss Leila Topping grew up, she became a concert pianist who traveled throughout Russia. (Chester Historical Society.)

Melrose Farms was originally part of the larger farm owned by John Sweazy, and was located near the location where Lowry Mead made his two-crop Riamede Farm with 1,000 apple trees and 2,000 peach trees. Melrose Farm was a poultry farm and eventually became Grace Bible Chapel. (John T. Wyckoff collection.)

Pictured here is one of the many "Horton houses" that was built in what the old-timers called "Hortontown"—because so many of the people in that area were from the Horton family. Later on it was to become known as the Gilbert Taylor Farm. (Gilbert Taylor Sr.)

Philip Weldh, who operated a general store near the crossroads, lived in, and most likely built, this home that was called "Robin Hurst." Some other families that have lived in this house, before it was torn down and replaced with the post office, were the Evans and the Searles. (Cliff Waters.)

This is an earlier photograph of "Stone Hedge Farm," one of the parcels of land that Mr. and Mrs. Alfred G. Kay purchased in Chester. The Kays also referred to the property as "Hidden River Farm." The sheep shed, garage, and barn (which had a badminton court inside) burned down when some electrical work was being done. This section of property is where the Kays had their drying room and the lab for their herb business. The property is now the Devereux Deerhaven facilities. (Martin Winkler.)

The bath house and swimming hole that the Kay family and their friends enjoyed was down along the Black River. The dam for the swimming hole was built in 1926. (Martin Winkler.)

The Kays moved "up on the hill" to this home in 1959. This building and surrounding property was donated to the Morris County Park Commission, and it also houses a chapter of The Nature Conservancy. (Martin Winkler.)

The small cottage pictured here was for the Kay's cook and was situated near the "Big House." (Martin Winkler.)

For over eight years in the 1930s, people came "from far and near" to enjoy the delicately herb-flavored food served at "The Herb Farm," located on today's State Park Road. Mrs. Alfred G. Kay started the tea room because of her fascination with herbs, and she not only grew all the herbs in her own gardens, but collected them from abroad as well. (Martin Winkler.)

Here we see Warren, Anita, and Audrey Kay picking herbs from their mother's garden. The Kays became the largest growers and producers of dried herbs, and soon carefully handled blends of herbs and vinegars were being packaged and sold under the trademark "Herb Farm." Martin Winkler, who worked for the Kays all his life, said that one year they planted over 13,000 plants. (Martin Winkler.)

This is the interior view of "The Herb Farm" tea room. It has been reported that such celebrities as Duncan Hines and Mary Margaret McBride came to enjoy the food at "The Herb Farm." (Martin Winkler.)

The mixing room was where the herbs would be blended together. Pictured here are Audrey Kay and Warren Kay (sitting), and Anita Kay (standing in the back). (Martin Winkler.)

Obadiah Seward came from Brookhaven, Long Island, in 1740, or earlier, and built this farmhouse, which still has the original seven fireplaces and wide floorboards. It was later called "The Welcome Home Farm." (John T. Wyckoff collection.)

General Nathan B. Cooper was to build the third Cooper home, his "mansion," in 1860. It is reported that this date is cut into the bricks under the northwest eaves. One interesting story of "the General" was that he was very tall and he had made for himself a bronze coffin—extra long and extremely heavy. The wagon-hearse bearing him to the Pleasant Hill Cemetery was to break down just across the Black River, leaving "the General" behind on the ground. (Chester Historical Society.)

There were a large number of beautiful homes in the Chester area. One of the most magnificent homes is that of well-known linen merchant Samuel C. Pullman (Pullman railroad cars). This elegant villa occupied one of the heights with a view which was not surpassed by any residence in the state. The villa burned down about 1960. (Chester Historical Society.)

This is the beautiful home of the Pitney-Jacobson Farm, which is now Hacklebarney Apple Orchard and Cider Mill. Pictured from left to right are Robert D. Pitney, Charlie, Elizabeth, Amy, Andy, Elwood, and unknown—all were Pitneys. (Wanda Jacobson.)

This is the log home of minuteman John Emmons. It later became the Wyckoff home. The Wyckoffs came from Readington Township in 1798, and farmed the orchards and land that the Emmons had owned. It has been noted in a letter in the Washington's Headquarters Museum Library in Morristown, written by Washington himself, that he had stayed in a log house one mile south of Chester. It was most likely this log house, because there are no records of any other log houses in that area. (Chester Historical Society.)

This is what the log house on Route 24, going toward Mendham, looked like in the 1930s. It was the business of Dr. Kay for awhile, and really has not changed much over the years. (Joan S. Case.)

It was around 1823 when Stephen R. Haines built his woolen mill down river from the Milltown gristmill. A few years later, William Nicholas, from Mendham, purchased the entire woolen mill enterprise and bought, or built, the house pictured here, which was across the road from the mill. The home and business were to remain in his family for several generations. (Chester Historical Society.)

In 1827, John Drake acquired 8 acres of land between Main Street and Budd Avenue for $800 and built his home in a classic center-hall fashion. The home was heated by the fireplaces and had a working kitchen hearth and oven. This image is a reversed print. (Chester Historical Society.)

The "Rockefeller's General Store" stood on the foundation seen here, until it burned down in 1913. The house beyond the foundation was the Rockefeller's family home. (Margaret Ardin.)

This is the main house of the "Echo Farm" around the turn of the century. Chester P. Apgar Jr. was born in this home. The farm is now called "Hideaway Farm." It belongs to the Mennen family, and is presently being farmed by the Kurt Alstede family. (Ann Apgar.)

This photograph, taken on June 15, 1929, shows the Swackhammer family home, which is on Pleasant Hill. (Chester Historical Society.)

At one time, Jacob Furrer worked for Mr. Searles at "Robin Hurst" and lived one winter in a tent while a house was being built for him on Fairmount Avenue. This home is on the property that was once part of "Robin Hurst," and a descendent of the Searles family stills resides here today. (Cyrilla Van Stone.)

The long-forgotten home of the E. Wortman family, who lived between Chester and Pottersville, stands, waiting for someone to come along and fix it up. In 1899, the Wortman's owned and cultivated 224 acres of farmland—most of which was planted in peaches. Their orchards were among the best in the county. (Chester Historical Society.)

This is a side view of the Wortman home. Peaches from the Wortman Farm were carted to Pottersville daily and shipped out on the Rockaway Valley Railroad, which was affectionately called the "Rockaby baby," because of its uneven roadbed. Chester was a great peach-producing area, until the San Jose scale killed all of the trees in the early 1900s. (Chester Historical Society.)

Five

CHURCH AND STATE

This building was once the Baptist church in Bedminster, and it was purchased in 1854 by the Newark Conference of the Methodist Episcopal Church. It was moved to Chester during the winter of 1880–81, and it became the original Methodist Episcopal church in the village. In 1911, when the new church was built on Main Street, this building housed the municipal offices. (John T. Wyckoff collection.)

The First Congregational Church was organized in 1740. The first house of worship was built near this site in 1747. The second, built in 1803, was located in the cemetery, where there are no gravestones today. The church, as we see it here, was built in 1856, and the interior is one of perhaps two remaining example of "trompe l'oeil" decorations in the state. (Gilbert Taylor Sr.)

This home sits adjacent to the First Congregational Church and is now the parsonage for the church. This former home of the Cyphers was acquired when the parsonage at Main Street was sold after World War II. (Herman Rademacher.)

At Chester's centennial celebration, on January 29, 1899, the town celebrated in style. On Monday evening, January 30, at the Congregational church, which had been made ready with the elaborate and beautiful decorations pictured above, there was held a program that lasted over three hours. The Chester Cornet Band made its first appearance on this occasion, and, from the porch of the church, greeted all comers with its fine strains of music. (John T. Wyckoff collection.)

One direct result of gas rationing was the birth of the Catholic church in Chester. Mr. and Mrs. Walter Serbe offered the use of their home, which was used as the church for nine years. The first mass was said there in June 1941. On Easter Sunday, 1950, the first mass was celebrated in the new church (pictured above), which was located across the street from the Serbe's home. This building eventually became the Borough Municipal Building. (Ken Urban.)

This was one of the many schools that Chester had. It is the Milldale School, which now serves as the Chester Township Municipal Building. It has been reported that it was once owned by the local Ku Klux Klan, before the municipality bought it. (Ann Apgar.)

Mr. Adolph Borie lived at lower Hacklebarney, and in 1924, Mr. Borie donated 190 acres of land to the state for a park. The park has Black River, weathered rocks and boulders, a 600-foot gorge, and other remnants of pre-glacial periods. During the Depression of the 1930s, the Civilian Conservation Corps removed the remains of miners' houses at Hacklebarney and used the materials to construct the field house at the park. (Howard Sutton Jr.)

74

"Your taxes for Chester Township" are shown here for the year 1873. (Chester Historical Society.)

M __*Harriet A. Miller*__

Your Taxes for Chester Township
FOR THE YEAR 1873.
Now due and payable to me, are as follows:

Number of Acres........................... *20*
Valuation of Real Estate is......$ *800*
Personal Property............... *100*
Debts..........................
Amount of Levy............... $ *100*
                              $

Poll Tax..$ *1 00*
State Tax..................... 87c per $1,000   *77*
County Tax................... $2.07 " "   *186*
School Tax................... 1.49 " "   *134*
District Tax.........................
Township Tax................. 52c " "   *47*
Road Tax..................... 2.04 " "   *184*
Dog Tax...................... 1.50

      Total..................... $ *6 20*

Paid *Chas S Emmons*   Collector   *7 0*

Dated

Now due and payable on or before the 20th of December, to CHARLES S. EMMONS, Collector.

The Commissioners of Appeal meet on the 4th Tuesday of November next, at the Chester House, at 10 o'clock A. M.

For the convenience of Tax Payers, I will be at the following named places, from 1 till 4 o'clock P. M. : At William Sharp's, on Saturday, Dec. 13th ; at Stephen Worthman's, on Monday, Dec. 15th ; at John H. Vandever's store, on Tuesday, Dec. 16th ; at Caleb G. Woodhull's store, on Wednesday, Dec. 17th ; at John Riggott's, on Thursday, Dec. 18th ; and at the Chester House, on Friday, Dec. 19th.

☞ Twelve per cent. interest will be added on all taxes not paid on or before the 20th of December, 1873.

Tax payers will present this notice to be receipted at payment.

CHAS. S. EMMONS, Collector.

Pictured here is Main Street looking west. Many of the buildings along Main Street not only housed general stores and luncheonettes, but a few of them also held the position of being the local post office or telephone offices. (Chester Historical Society.)

FEDERATED CHURCH AND CHAPEL.
C1851), CHESTER,N.J.

About 1750, William Larison donated a piece of land at the crest of Pleasant Hill for a church and burying ground for the Presbyterian congregation. This was the home for the congregation until 1851, when 2.5 acres on Main Street (pictured here) were purchased for $247.50. The adjoining parsonage property was to be added in 1859 for $200. The old church on the hill came down, but the cemetery stayed with a new name—Pleasant Hill Cemetery. (Ann Apgar.)

The Rev. William Woodhull was a graduate from Princeton in 1763, and was filling the pulpit in Brookhaven, Long Island, when the Presbyterians sent out a call for him to come and lead their church. The call was accepted in 1765, and the Rev. Woodhull served the church for a number of years, until he developed bronchial trouble and had to stop. He died in 1824, and is buried at Pleasant Hill Cemetery. (John T. Wyckoff collection.)

The Rev. Edward P. Gardner came to be the Presbyterian pastor, staying for eight years, during which time he wrote a history of the church. (John T. Wyckoff collection.)

After it was found that the ground behind the new church on Main Street was unsuitable for a burial ground, it was decided to keep the old graveyard on the hill, but to have it independent of the church, and to incorporate it under the new name, "Pleasant Hill Cemetery." In the beginning, burial plots were sold for $5–$25 each. In 1903, the stone chapel was built at a cost of $3,000. (Ann Apgar.)

The first "preacher" assigned to the Chester Methodist Church, in 1868, was Caleb A. Lippincott, who was considered "one of the best-known Methodist preachers in Morris County." Methodist services had been held in the village academy, until 1881, when this new church was brought up to its new location from Bedminster, being pulled in large sections by six mule teams. It was also used for municipal offices and is now the Black River Playhouse. (John T. Wyckoff collection.)

The new Methodist church was built on Main Street in 1908, and served that congregation until 1921, when it burned down. The churches in Chester joined together in 1918, largely for economic reasons. They called it the "Federated Church of Chester," and each retained its own denominational affiliation, until two years later, when the Congregationalists voted to withdraw. This arrangement continued until the Methodist church burned down and was absorbed into what came to be the "Community Presbyterian Church." (Ann Apgar.)

Here is a view of the inside of the Methodist church, as it stood on Main Street, until it burned down in 1921. (John T. Wyckoff collection.)

This is an outside view of the Methodist church on Main Street on a Sunday morning. The Methodist church never had a parsonage, but it rented houses for married preachers, and boarding places for single ones. (Ann Apgar.)

Pictured here is the original Methodist church that was brought up from Bedminster. When the new church on Main Street was built in 1910, the Township of Chester purchased the old church building for $550. The township community held its first meeting in 1911, and at some time the small, shoemaker shop building was moved from East Main Street to Maple Avenue, behind the township hall, to use as a jail. The hall was also used for social gatherings, plays, and picture shows. (Chester Historical Society.)

Pictured here is a collage of the men who ran the Borough of Chester in 1939. (Margaret Ardin.)

Six

READING, WRITING, AND . . .

From about the time of the Civil War to the early 1900s, there were seven school districts in Chester, with a school for each. Pictured here is Pleasant Hill School District Number Five, which was in operation until 1919. Some of the students are posing for pictures in front of their school. (Pat Pedersen.)

Caleb Horton came from Southold and bought property in Chester in 1748. Portions of that land are still in the Horton family today. David L. Horton donated a piece of that land for a new Forest Hill School, built in 1866 (pictured here). This was school district number one, and Miss Paine was the teacher. (Bob Horton.)

The "Cross Roads" Stone Schoolhouse was erected September 15, 1830, and still looks much as it did years ago—although it now serves as a very attractive home. The building seems to have been jointly owned at one time. The upper story was used as a Congregational meetinghouse, and the lower room was the schoolhouse. This was school district number two, and Josephine Langdon was the teacher. (Chester Historical Society.)

Main St. & Chester House, Chester, N. J.

Early in the decade, Daniel Budd and Theodore Perry Skellenger purchased the Chester Brick Hotel for $3,650, with a fine new school in mind called the Chester Institute. Mr. William Rankin was the principal. Later on, Daniel Budd decided there were too many rough mining men loitering near the school for the good of the young ladies, so he built a stone, 26-room house for the use of the institute. (Chester Historical Society.)

Books free for everybody, right at the door—
if you vote "Yes."

Pictured here, on a postcard advertisement, is a "book mobile" that traveled to Chester. The book mobile ad read, "books free for everybody, right at the door—if you vote yes." (John T. Wyckoff collection.)

In compliance with the state law of 1829, school districts were created in Chester. Some of the original ones were the Chester Academy (on the hill); Milltown District (also called "Sugartown"), which was a small stone building on Parker Road and Schoolhouse Lane; and the Masonic District on Peapack Road. The school pictured here is the Grove Street School. (Ann Apgar.)

This is a school portrait of the students attending the Grove Street School. None of them were able to be identified. (Chester Historical Society.)

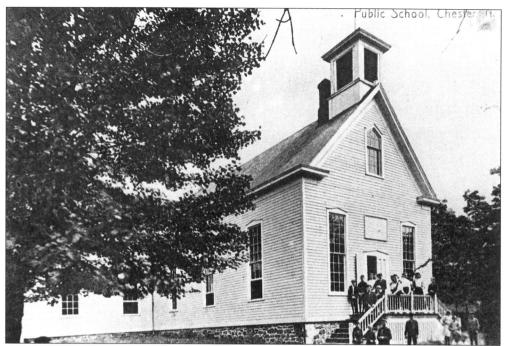

Pictured here is a front view of the Grove Street School, with a group of students posing for pictures. This school has now been divided into two separate buildings. The buildings are located next to each other and are currently used to house four apartments. (Ken Urban.)

This is an old school portrait taken at the Milldale School District, which is now the Chester Township Municipal Building. None of the students or the teacher were able to be identified. (Chester Historical Society.)

Daniel Budd decided to move his Chester Institute to his fine, stone, 26-room house on New Street, for not only the use of the institute, but also for his family to live in. It was a spacious, three-story house with a bell tower. There was a 20-by-30-foot classroom and two 20-by-20-foot rooms with concert grand pianos. Pictured here is the front view. (Ken Urban.)

Here we see the back of the Chester Institute with a good view of the bell tower. There was a free-standing, circular staircase in the gracious center hall which rose from the basement to the third floor. One account claims that in one year there were four hundred scholars—boarders and day students—enrolled. This building was torn down to make way for a shopping center in the early 1970s. (John T. Wyckoff collection.)

86

CHESTER INSTITUTE.

To *Miss Hattie Colley*

CARD OF STANDING,

For Term Ending *July 28, 1865*

Geography 7⅔	*Oral Spelling 8*
Arithmetic 8	
Grammar 8¼	*Literary Exercises. 8½*

DEMERIT.   DEPORTMENT. *Good*

MERIT —The Scale of Merit ranges from 1 to 10   Note 5 is inferior; from 5 to 7 is good; from 7 to 8 is very good; from 8 to 9, superior, and from 9 to 10, very superior.

DEMERIT.—Each Demerit mark diminishes deportment from 1 to 3, according to gravity of offence. Each mark requires an explanation; 5 marks, public reproof; 8, probation; 10, dismission from school. *L B Stoutenburgh Prin,*

This is an 1865 "card of standing" from the Chester Institute. Miss Hattie Colley did not do too badly. (Ann Apgar.)

Originally a home, built before 1790, this building doubled as the Masonic building and the Mount Rose School District Number Four on Chester-Gladstone Road. A few of the people have been identified as, from left to right: (front row) third is Dorothy Henderson, fourth is Stanley Bodine, sixth is Ike (?); (middle row) first is Lucy Boyle, fourth is Mel Blaufuss, seventh is Dudley Bragg (the teacher). (Martin Winkler Jr.)

The old Milldale School on Parker Road, now the Chester Township Municipal Building, was so extensively remodeled in 1967 that the original structure is no longer recognizable. The old schoolhouse was once owned by the local Ku Klux Klan, prior to its purchase by the municipality in the 1930s. (Gilbert Taylor Sr.)

This is a school portrait of the teacher and students that attended the Hacklebarney School District Number Seven (1871–1917). The school was located on the comers of Pottersville Road and Hacklebarney Road. Pictured here, from left to right, are Essie Wortman, Ruth Hildebrandt Larison, Mahlon H. Pitney, Mary Call Skellenger (teacher), Lloyd Hildebrandt, Laura Hildebrandt, and Bertha Hildebrandt. (Wanda Jacobson.)

The new Chester Public School opened in 1925, with Charles Williamson (whom the school is now named after) as principal, and Elizabeth Keller, Emarilla Van Fleet, and Dudley Bragg as teachers. Charles A. Williamson was the administrator of the Chester Schools for 37 years, until he retired in 1956. (Ann Apgar.)

CHESTER PUBLIC SCHOOL

DISTRICT No. 66.

ROOM NO. 1.

School Report of _Hattie Smith_

for month ending _Sept 26" 1890_

No. of days attendance .... _20_

No. lessons recited .. _75_..., missed .._0_....

No. of times late .... _0_

Deportment .... _10_

J. B. F. Smith ......Parent.

C. M. Kiser ......Teacher.

Miss Hattie Smith seems to have done well on her report card from the Chester Public School. (Ann Apgar.)

This is a third-grade photograph taken at the Chester Public School, located on Main Street, on September 15, 1930. From left to right are as follows: (first row) second is Doris Croot Hoffman, fourth is Earl Jacobus, fifth is Edna Koller, and seventh is Grace Mercandante; (second row) first is Jeanette Williamson, second is Margaret Smith, third is Ginny De Hart Breitweiser, fourth is Margaret Dorimus, sixth is Russell Apgar, and eighth is Alfred Wyckoff; (third row) first is Helen Nunn and seventh is Fred Wyckoff; (fourth row) first is Gladys Shann, second is Clifford Gellespie, third is Dorothy Fleming, and seventh is John T. Wyckoff. (Joan S. Case.)

Pictured here is Joyce Gray Wyckoff, getting off the school bus at the Cooper Grist Mill area and getting ready for the more than one-mile walk home. (John T. Wyckoff collection.)

Lois "Tommy" Barker always got good grades while in school. Here is part of a report card from school year 1934–35, signed by her teacher, Mr. Dudley Bragg. (Lois "Tommy" Barker.)

CHESTER
PUBLIC SCHOOL

CHESTER TOWNSHIP SCHOOL DISTRICT
CHESTER, NEW JERSEY

REPORT OF

Lois Barker

Grade ..6.............. School Year..*1934–35*...

"Going to school is a business which demands regular attendance and promptness."

TO PARENT OR GUARDIAN

This report card is to inform the parent or guardian of the pupils progress in school work and to secure cooperation from those at home in order that the best possible results may be obtained from the pupil.

CHARLES A. WILLIAMSON,
Principal.

Dudley K. H. Bragg Teacher

The 1944 eighth-grade class of the Chester Public School is pictured here with Charles Williamson—not only the school's principal, but also this class's teacher. Pictured here are, from left to right, as follows: (front row—girls) Luella Thornton, Elanore Nass, Jean Leck, Evelyn Stroud, Elvira Filiberto, Alice Dunn, Clem Robinson, Joyce Gray Wyckoff, Jeannie Cowie Forsythe, and Phyliss Furrier; (back row—boys) Charles Williamson, Albert ?, Fred Shann, Billy Seals, Eddie Kappas, Herman Rademacher, Walter Conklin, Harry Emmons, Donald Romeline, and Ray Croot. (Joyce Gray Wyckoff.)

This is a school photograph of the Milltown School, in 1905. The students are identified below. (Both images Township of Chester.)

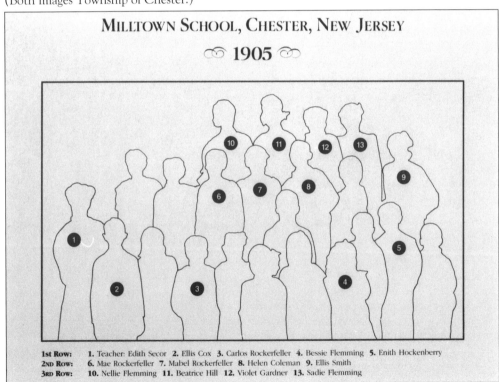

MILLTOWN SCHOOL, CHESTER, NEW JERSEY
∽ 1905 ∽

1st Row: 1. Teacher: Edith Secor 2. Ellis Cox 3. Carlos Rockerfeller 4. Bessie Flemming 5. Enith Hockenberry
2nd Row: 6. Mae Rockerfeller 7. Mabel Rockerfeller 8. Helen Coleman 9. Ellis Smith
3rd Row: 10. Nellie Flemming 11. Beatrice Hill 12. Violet Gardner 13. Sadie Flemming

Seven

ALWAYS THERE
WHEN NEEDED

This is the Chester Volunteer Fire Company's first group photograph, taken in the late 1920s or early 30s. October 1921 was the first official meeting of the Chester Volunteer Fire Company Number One. It was held in the home of member Lloyd Tredway. Pictured here are: (sitting on the bumper) John Fragamane and Ray Croot; (kneeling) Paul Sutton, George Dosa, and Charles Skellinger; (left of the truck) Alvin Martenis, unknown, and Bill Furrier; (on top of the truck, from left to right) Walt Barkman, unknown, Bill Strait, Duke Hartwell, Alvin Van Fleet and Austin Nichols (both sitting behind the steering wheel); (standing) Everett Vanover and Charles Sharp; (standing to the right of the truck) Ted Cavanough, Tom Barker, Bill Cramer, ? Bodine, Lloyd Tredway, Buldger Blaine, and Bill Sturganger. (Chester Volunteer Fire Department.)

In 1923, the first firehouse was a 20-foot-by-30-foot wooden building, constructed on land where the present firehouse now stands, with labor furnished by the members, under the supervision of member J.C. Hoffman. The first fire alarm was fashioned from a railroad engine wheel and is now mounted, and still stands, in the park by the firehouse. The alarm was sounded by striking the rim with a sledge hammer. (Gilbert Taylor Sr.)

In 1935, preliminary steps for construction of a new firehouse were taken, and in 1940, the new firehouse was completed. The first meeting was held here in November. Mr. John S. Wyckoff did the mason work, and in the bottom right-hand corner of the building was placed a cornerstone with 1940 engraved on it and dated papers inside a capsule behind the cornerstone. (John T. Wyckoff collection.)

94

In 1950, a single-story addition was added on the north side of the firehouse, and in 1962, another single-story addition was built on the south side of the firehouse. In 1922, the first apparatus was constructed by mounting a chemical tank on a Pierce Arrow chassis, and a small electric siren was mounted across the street on the roof of Green's drugstore. (Louis L. Case.)

Pictured here is the dedication of the laying of the cornerstone in the new firehouse, built in 1940. Those in the picture have been identified as Edwin Collis (holding a hat), William Tredway (at the front and right), and the young boy is Walt Conklin. Standing from left to right are Rev. Lemmon, Muriel Conklin Lutz, Irene Zurcher, Grace Barkman, Lulu O'Dell, Helen Stelce, unknown man in the back, Millie Barkman, Caroline O'Dell, Vernon Parks, unknown, Jack Hoffman, and Bill Blaine. (Chester Volunteer Fire Department.)

This group shot was taken at one of the Fourth of July celebrations that the Chester Fire Company was always famous for, c. 1945. Only a few of the men have been identified, and they are Edwin Collis, Al O'Brien, and Herman Rademacher. Every year there would be crowds of people lined up along the streets to view the wonderful parades that the firemen would organize. (Louis L. Case.)

This photograph was taken in 1951, and the members of the first aid squad and the fire department have been identified, from left to right, as follows: (front row, kneeling) Arnold Martenis, Paul Sutton, Reuben Thompson, George McFarren, Walt Patrie, Kenneth O'Dell, Herman Clausen, and Herman Rademacher; (middle row) unknown, Warren Kay, Gert Dean, Millie Barkman, unknown, unknown, Art Lee, unknown, Irvin Tredway, Leroy "Shorty" Nunn, and Charlie Williamson; (back row) Emile Ardin, Tom Dean, unknown, unknown, unknown, unknown, Lee Case, Jack Hoffman, unknown, Al O'Brien, and unknown. (Chester Volunteer Fire Department.)

This photograph was probably shot in the late 1940s, and pictures the following, from left to right: (kneeling) Tom Dean, unidentified, Mahlon Pitney, Art Lee, Boldger Blane, Leroy "Shorty" Nunn, and Herman Clausen; (back row) Herman Rademacher, Vernon Parks, Irvin Tredway, Arnold Martenis, Jack Hoffman, and Lee Case. (Chester Volunteer Fire Department.)

Bob Cole donated an old hearse for the first aid squad. Pictured here is Millie Barkman, Buldger Blaine, and Myrtle Martenis. The fire company set up operation procedures for a fire company-sponsored first aid squad in 1945. Due to insurance problems, membership in the first aid squad would be restricted to members of the fire company. (Chester Volunteer Fire Department.)

This photograph of the Chester Volunteer Fire Company was taken on July 4, 1949. Pictured here are, from left to right, as follows: (front row) fifth is Charlie Tredway, sixth is Lee Case, and ninth is Charles Williamson; (middle row) fifth is Hank Hoffman; (back row) third is Al O'Brien and fourth is Jack Hoffman. (Louis L. Case.)

This photograph of the Ladies Auxiliary was taken on July 4, 1949. Pictured here are, from left to right, Sara Sliker, Lulu O'Dell, Anna Williamson, Madeline Steinberg, Muriel Blaine, Mrs. Buldger Blaine, Beatrice Wyckoff Case, Greta Nunn, and three unknown individuals. (Louis L. Case.)

This wonderful farmhouse-turned-tavern was built in 1752 at the northeast corner of the "crossroads," and was aptly-named "The Cross Roads Inn." The entire town was sad on Monday evening, November 26, 1962, when it burned to the ground, in spite of the efforts of 11 fire companies with 25 pieces of equipment. All that was left were parts of outside walls, some bits of jewelry, and a $20 bill. Rumor has it that one of the locals still has the spittoon from the tavern. (John T. Wyckoff collection.)

Pictured here is the Chester Volunteer Fire Company's first fire engine, which was built in 1921. The retired engine was carried through the streets of Chester during one of the many parades that the fire company sponsored. (Ann Apgar.)

Marching here, in one of Chester's Fourth of July parades, is Jean Anderson Steinberg. (Ann Apgar.)

Coming down Maple Avenue (originally called "Mud Street") were many of the local farmers, driving their tractors. (Ann Apgar.)

To start off each Fourth of July parade, firemen would carry the U.S. flag and the fire company's flag. This photograph was shot on Main Street, with Leck's Luncheonette in the background. (Louis L. Case.)

Sitting back on their front porch, ready to enjoy one of Chester's parades, are the Chester P. Apgar family and the Charles Williamson family. Seen here, from left to right, are Henry Jackson, Mrs. Anna Williamson, Alberta Gouldey, Daisy Emmons, Chester Apgar Sr., Mrs. Jackson, Charles Williamson, Paul Apgar, and Charlie Emmons. (Ann Apgar.)

July 4, 1948, was the date of this parade. Here we see some of the Chester Fire Company's equipment driving down Main Street, in front of The Chester House. (Ann Apgar.)

Coming down Church Street in the 1949 July Fourth Parade is the first firetruck the company owned. (Ann Apgar.)

The Chester parades were so popular that people would come from all over the area to line the streets so they could view the procession. The Centennial Building stands in the background. (Ann Apgar.)

Crowds are packed in around the Chester House to view the parades. (Ann Apgar.)

Here is a 1949 Chester parade float, modeled after "The Centennial Building" that Chester P. Apgar owned. (Clara Ammerman.)

At this Chester parade are, from left to right, Clara O'Dell Ammerman, Helen Jacobson Gueren, and Paulanita Beam, walking down Main Street. (Clara Ammerman.)

A Chester parade moves along Main Street, by the old post office and Chester House. (Township of Chester.)

Pictured here we see Post 216B Aircraft Warning Service Men from Chester in one of the Fourth of July parades along Main Street. Clinton Mack and Joseph Croot are holding the sign. Dudley Bragg, unidentified, Paul Apgar, and Tom Dean appear in the second row. (Mrs. Percy Chubb.)

This is the Bernardsville Fire Department marching in one of Chester's parades. (John T. Wyckoff.)

The Chester parades always ended with the horseback riders. These riders are coming up Grove Street, alongside the French restaurant. (Mrs. Percy Chubb.)

The Washington Camp Number Eight of the Patriotic Order Sons of America was organized by William E. Cary and George E. Conover and instituted on August 5, 1895. Here the organization is marching in the parade on Decoration Day, May 30, 1914. (John T. Wyckoff collection.)

Bus Crum and an unknown individual are riding on a float in another one of Chester's parades. (Am Apgar.)

Here the Chester Volunteer Fire Department is marching in one of Booton's parades. A few of the marchers have been identified as, from left to right, Martin Winkler (holding the United States flag), Reuben Thompson, Irvin Tredway, Art Lee, and Jack Hoffman. (Chester Volunteer Fire Department.)

Lee Case is waiting to enter the parade on this Farmall tractor, which is pulling a float. (Ann Apgar.)

Eight

MAILS, RAILS, AND DOWN THE TRAILS

Mr. Van Fleet received his appointment from the postal inspector and started delivery of the mail on May 15, 1906. The new carrier used a horse-drawn buggy and sleigh until late in 1907, when he bought a cab. Pictured here, with Mr. Van Fleet and his "cozy cab," are Nathan and Lewis Horton. (Chester Historical Society.)

The post office, in 1906, was located in this small building called "Rockefeller Center," which was near the firehouse. Mr. Van Fleet served under three postmasters: Lawyer Smith, Alonzo P. Green, and Austin Thompson. (Chester Historical Society.)

This is how Mr. Van Fleet would have to deliver Christmas mail in the early days. Civil service regulations compelled Mr. Van Fleet to retire in 1940, after nearly 35 years of service. (Chester Historical Society.)

No. ___5-1___ Post Office, CHESTER, NEW JERSEY

_____JUL 1 1914_____, 191

M._____ W Smith _____ 9 3

To **RENT OF BOX No.** _____ for Quarte

ding _____, 191 , $ 15C

Received payment,

ING THIS BILL WITH YOU.

See Regulations on other side.   Postmaster.

This is a receipt from July 1, 1914, for a post office box rental in the amount of 15¢, and signed by Alonzo P. Green, who was the postmaster. (Chester Historical Society.)

Black River, for which the town of Chester was originally named, was used for many purposes, such as for power to run the mills, for fishing, for boating, etc. (Township of Chester.)

Pictured here are some great old cars from earlier in this century. These fellows must have appreciated not having to ride their horses to the taverns in town anymore. They are parked in front of the Chester House. (Gilbert Taylor Sr.)

An unidentified individual is shown here taking a stroll over the bridge by the "Lower Hacklebarney Mill." (Chester Historical Society.)

This is the bridge and the dam on Black River, near the Cooper Grist Mill. (Ann Apgar.)

Back in the late 1800s, if the wagon or carriage did not need fixing, the horses still needed shoeing. (John T. Wyckoff collection.)

Out for a drive in the horse and buggy on a cold winter's day, down by the "Lower Hacklebarney Mill." (John T. Wyckoff collection.)

This is Mr. Martin Winkler, who was the caretaker for the Kay Estate, and his dog "Prince." (Martin Winkler Jr.)

Seeing a need for better transportation of the ore that was being mined in the Chester area, Daniel Budd, the state director of the Camden and Amboy Railroad (New Jersey's first), did something about it. It was largely through his influence that the Chester Railroad was built. The road was built by the Chester Railroad Company, which was an "adjunct" of the Morris & Essex Railroad (later D.L. & W.), from Dover to Chester, with six stations in between. (Gilbert Taylor Sr.)

This train pulled out of the "Muskrat Station" (D.L. & W.). The first train, known as the "tree train," ran January 2, 1869, with Marshall Sayre as conductor. Marshall Abram Sayre is identified as being the fifth man in from the left. (Township of Chester.)

This engine derailed at the turntable at the D.L. & W. Station in Chester. Back in those days, they had to get out of the engine and drive all of the livestock from the tracks. It was noted that the Hoboken-to-Chester run was especially bad. (Township of Chester.)

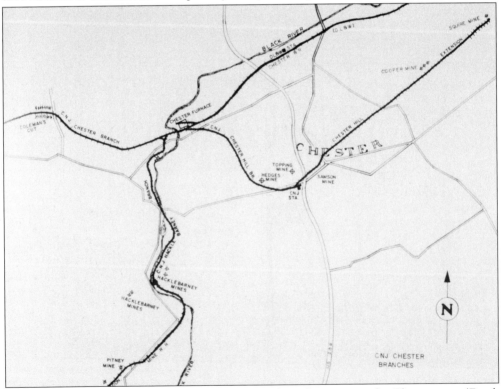

This is a map with the locations of the different tracks and stations in the Chester area. (Frank Carey.)

What the High Bridge Railroad called its Chester Branch was apparently the line that ran through Long Valley, past the Chester Furnace, terminating at the Chester Railroad (pictured here). The High Bridge Road was built as a feeder to the Central Railroad of New Jersey, intended primarily for shipping iron ore. (John T. Wyckoff collection.)

Two stations were built, one at the Chester Furnace and one at the Chester Hill, which is pictured here. In this station yard were tracks, a coal yard, and a freight office. Trains backed from Chester toward Long Valley. The first train was run from High Bridge to Chester on July 1, 1876, with Samuel Crook as conductor. (Frank Carey.)

117

Pictured here is a view of the D.L. & W. Station at Muskrat. It was noted that originally, Daniel Budd wanted the railroad to come right into the village, behind the hotel of which he owned, but that General Cooper had won out with his wish to have it a mile away. (Chester Historical Society.)

The rectangular building in the center and the scale house to the right were connected with the coal and lumber business, operated by station master Harry Cyphers. (Herman Rademacher.)

Seen here is a 1915 photograph of the D.L. & W. Station and one of its passenger trains. (Frank Carey.)

This is the Central Railroad Culvert going toward the Chester Furnace. (Chester Historical Society.)

RETURNING

Lackawanna Railroad | DELAWARE LACKAWANNA & WESTERN R·R

GOOD ONLY IN DIRECTION INDICATED

DOVER to CHESTER

Good only **THIRTY DAYS** from date of sale as indicated by stamp on back. No stop-over allowed. Liability for loss of or damage to baggage shall not exceed $1 per lb.

3 **9369**

(S29)

EXC. *Geo. M. Cullen* Passenger Traffic Man...

Here is a ticket for a returning trip from Dover to Chester on the Delaware, Lackawanna, & Western Railroad. (Ann Apgar.)

Lackawanna Railroad | DELAWARE LACKAWANNA & WESTERN R·R

CHESTER to NEW YORK

Good only one day from date of sale as indicated by stamp on back. Void if detached from and subject to conditions as specified on Return Coupon.

200

EXC.

GOING TRIP

This ticket, dated July 13, 1903, was good for a "going trip" from Chester to New York on the D.L. & W. Railroad. (Ann Apgar.)

The Chester Furnace was built in 1878 on Furnace Road by the Jersey Spiegel Iron Company. It was a blast furnace which was meant to make Spiegel-eisen out of the residue of Franklinite, after the zinc had been extracted. It was abandoned almost immediately, and the furnace was leased to the W.J. Taylor and Company, of High Bridge. There were one hundred men employed, and it was a successful blast furnace for a number of years. (John T. Wyckoff collection.)

During the mining days in Chester, this Hacklebarney trestle brought the ore to the waiting gondola cars for shipment to the blast furnaces. No traces remain of this testament to Chester's glorious past, because an early morning fire on June 13, 1885, destroyed the trestle and wooden enclosures. (John T. Wyckoff collection.)

Sometime in the 1890s, the proud crew of this Chester engine paused to have their picture taken at the Chester depot. Built by Dickson in 1872, the engine was still trim and shiny more than 20 years later and served the Lackawanna well until 1902. (John T. Wyckoff collection.)

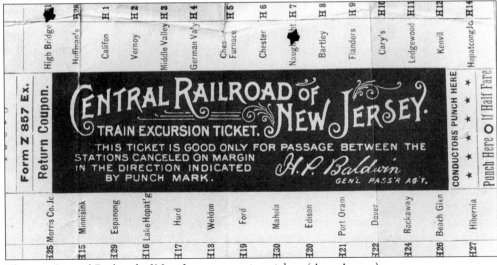

This is a Central Railroad of New Jersey excursion ticket. (Ann Apgar.)

This section of the Chester Railroad, which went from Long Valley to Chester, was known as "Coleman's Cut." (John T. Wyckoff collection.)

A favorite Sunday afternoon pastime was "walking the tracks," from Chester to Long Valley, to visit with friends. Pictured here is Jennie Wyckoff. (Joan S. Case.)

Another fun way of getting around was on horseback. Pictured here is Lindley G. Cook, who did quite a lot for the 4-H club. (Doris Hoffman.)

Here is the local bread man, Roy Swackhammer from German Valley, who would deliver fresh bread to the residents of Chester. (Chester Historical Society.)

Pictured here is the local milk delivery man for the Chester area. Milk delivery is still available in the area today. (Chester Historical Society.)

Another fun way to get around was in a pony and carriage. Pictured here are Charlie Leck (the smallest boy), Johnny Steinberg (the boy with the reins), and Harold Lewin. (John T. Wyckoff collection.)

Mr. Peter's bus picked up the schoolchildren and took them to the Williamson School on Main Street in the 1940s. The building in the back sits on Route 24, between Chester and Mendham, and used to house Leo Norton's appliance store. (John T. Wyckoff collection.)

This is the long and winding road from Milldale up to Chester. Pictured to the left is the old Rockefeller General Store. (John T. Wyckoff collection.)

Everyone helps in digging out from the massive snow storms back in the 1940s. This photo was taken along Pottersville Road in Chester. (Cliff Waters.)

The snow could sure become deep back in the 1940s. (Cliff Waters.)

Learning to ride their ponies on the Kay Estate are Anita and Audrey Kay. With them is their father, Alfred G. Kay, and Fred Jordan. (Martin Winkler Jr.)

Countless people have traveled up the Main Street of Chester by walking, biking, riding horses, and driving in carriages and cars.